BEING SINGLE

DEBUNK THE MYTHS & FIND HAPPINESS

Sukhi Kaur

Being Single:
Exploding the Myths and Finding Happiness

This book is dedicated to:

My parents and siblings.

My friends Bal and Angela who have been the best supportive friends anyone could have asked for.

To my precious Nani ji, whose love, prayers and strength have guided me to live my best life.

Lastly, this book is dedicated to every single person out there – remember, you are enough. I wrote this for you.

FOREWORD

I started writing about my singlehood journey more than ten years ago when I began journaling each date I went on. It was journaling that helped me to understand myself when things weren't going as planned. I had lost friends close to me, and had had my heart broken, but, during those moments where I saw no light at the end of the tunnel, I was becoming myself. I was on a journey of self-discovery again, and I really wanted to find stories from women that looked like me, who had gone through the emotions and experiences I had gone through. I needed another single woman, preferably from the same culture, to share her story, and tell me about the joy of single life, but I couldn't find her.

In the culture I belong to, singlehood is seen as a failure, but when I look at my own journey, that's not what I see.

I was having a pretty hard time navigating the single path. All I heard was:

'Are you picky?'

'You're not trying hard enough.'

'You're too independent.'

Everyone around me seemed to be getting married and having children, while I was just figuring out my meal plan for the following week, what new gym exercises I wanted to try out, and where my next holiday was going to be. It was hard to fit in the search for Mr. Right on top of all of that!

I read so much conflicting advice - play hard to get, don't be too eager, don't "pick" up the bill, don't make the first move. It made my head spin - all I wanted was to find a decent man with whom I could have a proper conversation and share a nice meal.

Other advice centered around what to do once you had a potential man in your sights – all focused on making him happy. But I don't want to play games or dress a certain way; I'm happy the way I am.

Then the penny dropped. I didn't need to follow the crowd and try and be like everyone else. I just needed to take my time knowing me and being comfortable in my skin. I don't want to pretend to be someone I'm not.

That's when I decided that just as I have had the courage to walk my path alone, I will have the courage to share my journey, and become a voice. That even if I inspire one woman, this was my purpose, and mission, and I made a difference to someone else's life.

The modern day single woman is far from someone who is sad, lonely and desperate. She should be applauded as being courageous enough to walk the path alone. She should be celebrated. We learn to wipe our own tears and walk a path confidently even when the storms come.

We have fallen, and risen several times, knowing the hard times made us stronger.

The single woman makes her own decisions, she is strong, she's learnt to be her own best friend. Some days are tough, but when she falls, she reminds herself she is enough.

The single woman is one of the bravest woman you will meet. She's probably had her heart broken many times. She asks herself, 'What am I doing? Where am I going?' She hasn't got everything figured out but she's the one whose inspired me to share my story. She is me and you.

This book will debunk some of the myths around singlehood and throw in a healthy dose of practical tips and hints you can apply to your own life. The aim is to give you a perspective on how to be single.

I am not an expert; I don't speak for other singletons and I'm not a representation of all Indian women, but I hope you'll find something here that resonates with you.

TABLE OF CONTENTS

THE DEFINITION OF SINGLEHOOD

S inglehood: A person who is unattached and not in a relationship or even dating. They are just that, single. However, there are different types of single people.

Type 1 is interested in dating or finding a partner, but they are happy as they are, and aren't fazed by the expectations of others. They're living their best life unapologetically.

Type 2 wants to find a partner, and has been through a series of unsuccessful dates, has been through moments of disappointment and sadness, have doubted themselves, felt alone and even cried.

Type 3 is single, and recovering from heartbreak or past relationships. They need to give themselves time to heal.

Type 4 is divorced. They might still be single because society judges them for being divorced, and so other singletons avoid dating them.

Type 5 is widowed and is making sense of the next chapter. They might be looking for love again, or they might stay single.

Type 6 has chosen to be single. They would rather be single than settle for someone who isn't right for them.

Type 7 has no intention of having a relationship, and is happy just to have no string attached sex.

Type 8 - has never been in any relationship and wants to experience being in one and having someone who cares for them and gives them love and affection.

Whatever the scenario, and there will be many more, each person within each type is different and will have had different experiences, and thus there is never one single reason for being single.

MYTH #1

You Must Get Married

Life is not just about finding Mr Right.

Life is about living your best life.

D o you look at the Instagram pictures of couples going on exotic holidays? Do you wish you had a jam-packed schedule for the weekend - taking the kids swimming or to clubs?

Remember - you can:

- Go on holiday
- Learn new things
- Take up an evening class
- Bake cookies on the weekend
- Give cuddles to all the people you love

1

- Watch movies all weekend

- Socialise

You can do any of these things on your own; it doesn't make you a sad or lonely person. What's so bad about baking cookies and sharing them with the people you love?

Being single doesn't mean there is no joy in your life; your life does not start when you find your "happy ending". Your path is about finding your own joy, and living your dream life, turning your dreams into your reality. How blessed are you to have a path, and all this time to yourself? Be unapologetic about living your best life. You get to choose what you want to do; you define your happy life. You are not defined by a status and you don't come with an expiry date.

Despite being unattached in a relationship, my schedule was full, working, meeting friends for dinner, a house to clean and dinner to make, not to mention the never-ending family functions with cousins and friends getting married. I was happy, and even managing to travel more, to get away for weekend trips. I didn't feel guilty about spending my Saturdays lounging around the house watching a box set. Or spending the whole day shopping, going into Debenhams having lunch, and a coffee and cake in Starbucks, returning home with a new lippy and different coloured eyeliners simply because I could afford it, and wanted to.

Single people can be happy and fulfilled. You can still live your best life.

Your happiness defines your success. Your status does not determine who you are. You represent who you are. Sometimes we hold onto some beliefs that might be ingrained in us, whether these come from our family, upbringing, culture, or even ourselves.

Ask yourself:

- What do I want?

- What will make me happy?

- Do I even want a relationship?

The world is changing. There are stories shared in the media about same-sex marriages, interracial marriages, mixed caste marriages. Marriage is a choice, and actually there are many people who choose to stay single and not get married. Women are no longer looking at men to provide for them, as they are now capable of living an independent life. Men are equally pursuing other passions.

Times have changed. There need to be more stories about single people also living their best lives - the reality is everyone is carving out their best experience, so carve yours and follow your path.

As a single person, you can buy your own home; you can have children and raise them on your own, without getting married, or even without a partner. You can travel alone, live alone, choose not to get married, choose not to have children, or even adopt.

People often marry because they want a partner and because they want children. Those two things don't necessarily lead to love, care, affection. Don't rush to find someone, tick marriage and children off your list and then find that you don't know yourself what you really want.

It's better to know yourself first - so love your single life.

Be mindful about your voice and tone and conduct when you're asked about your single status. Don't hang your head in shame, hold your head up high, and be unapologetic.

Let's face it, with divorce rates sky-high across all cultures and religions, it's obvious marriage is not all fairy tales and eternal happiness. Who can blame the single person for hesitating? It's not being "picky"'. We put all our trust in that one person when we say, "I do". But the reality is that couples get divorced, they cheat on each other, there can be abuse – physical and mental. It's wise to take your time, to know who you are and what you want, and to trust yourself before you trust others with your happiness.

Single people are multi-faceted and can live full lives beyond trying to find a partner. Being single does not mean you are broken.

MYTH #2

Is There Something Wrong With You?

Before you look for things that are wrong with you,

go inwards and discover all the things that are right with you

"When was your last relationship?"

He studied me suspiciously. I was at a speed dating event, opposite a rather handsome lawyer. We had three minutes to seal the deal and make it to date one. I was optimistic it was in the bag. I wanted to know more about him, the foreign countries he had visited, his weekend plans, what he did outside of work, and

I needed to crack on - the timer was ticking. Mr. Lawyer was too interested in finding out what was wrong with me.

"But you're pretty? You seem like a great girl. Why are you still single?"

His eyes were wide. He was leaning forward, a picture of frustration and surprise.

I took a deep breath, as I studied his face, before finally saying, 'I don't know... I just am.'

When I was single and approaching thirty, it's no exaggeration when I say I was asked hundreds of times why I was single. I enjoyed my life, cracking on with it, travelling for work - I seriously loved every aspect of my life; I wasn't worried about being single. Still, the very fact that I kept being asked this question made me wonder if they knew something I didn't.

The truth was I had been trying, but it was hard to meet someone while juggling everything else that was going on in my life. I didn't stop eating, dinner still needed to be made, I still had to work, still had bills to pay. Only internally those little voices would trigger a little spark of fear.

"Are you fussy?"

"Are you picky?"

"You best hurry up now, you're not getting any younger."

"Forget working now and your career. You're too independent, that's why you're not getting anywhere with men."

"You're going to intimidate guys if you're too career-minded and ambitious."

It was endless.

It got to me. I began questioning things. What was wrong with me? I had low self-esteem; I began to panic.

But then I started debunking those myths – because they are myths.

I stopped asking myself what was wrong with me and started celebrating all those things that are right with me instead.

MYTH#3

You Feel Sad and Alone

I declare a new definition for loneliness.

Your relationship status does not dictate that you are alone. The path you're walking alone will help you to know yourself. Your loneliness is your gift. Do not disturb the process.

Throughout my single years, there are many things I have done on my own such as:

- Gone to a coffee house, and enjoyed a hot chocolate.

- Travelled - yes, you learn how to carry the big suitcases and take it off the conveyer belt yourself while holding your handbag and hand luggage bag.

- Lived and worked abroad.

- Gone for a meal.

- Gone to the cinema.

- Gone for walks.

- Visited the gym.

- Taken a fitness class.

- Attended speed dating events.

- Gone on a spiritual retreat to India.

Whatever the journey has been, I have embraced every opportunity. Every change has been exciting and scary. I have just gone with it.

I used to worry what people would think if they saw me sitting on my own in a coffee shop or at the cinema. Would they think I was a billy-no-mates? But look around you – there are lots of people enjoying things by themselves.

The truth is, most people are concerned about themselves. They don't care what you're doing! I started to enjoy all this time I had. I enjoyed going out for early morning walks or sitting on the grass, reading my book. I enjoyed sitting in Starbucks, watching everyone running from place to place, while I was just there, just me and my thoughts.

Loneliness is open to a lot of interpretation. I know a lot of people who feel alone. They have it all, the beautiful house, kids, a husband or wife, yet they still felt empty inside. It's easy for people to assume that you must be feeling sad and alone because you are single. You must be depressed and low because you're not in a relationship. It's easy for people to question your path and even feel they can make comments about it when they don't know your journey. It's easy for people to judge you and make up their own opinion about why you might be single. But people don't have the right to put you under a magnifying glass.

From my experiences, it is human nature to feel sadness and disappointment when things don't go to plan. I have felt this with each passing year, and it hasn't always been easy. I have cried at times, but it's not because I was alone – I would rather be alone than be with the wrong person. It was because I didn't yet fully appreciate the person I was and the person I am. It was because society and my culture and the people around me made me feel like there was something wrong.

As I approached thirty, I felt myself transforming. I had a spiritual awakening. I found mindful meditation. I found something that gave me so much joy, it became my coping strategy.

This was the beginning of my journey to self-awareness.

When we look at life as a whole, there will be moments when you will be happy, and there will be moments when you are sad. What is the definition of true happiness, anyway? Everyone has their own definition of joy, and how they want to live their life. The truth is, it is human nature to experience pleasure as much as it is to experience sadness. Nothing ever stays the same, and things are continually changing. We are unaware of what's around the corner. So why dwell on something you can't change? Why not enjoy the path you're on? Why not go inwards and find your peace and do more of what makes you happy - based on your own definition and measure of happiness?

Singlehood means you didn't settle for just any relationship.

You are a bold woman who can confidently walk her path alone, without a partner.

You don't need to be rescued. Single people can live alone and provide for themselves.

I have learned to be my own best friend. I no longer feel alone, because I can survive alone.

That loneliness does not mean I'm alone. I realise I don't need validation from others, I only need to validate myself, and that's the greatest gift this journey has brought me.

Some Tips On How To Embrace This Path You're Navigating:

- Use this time to mature and grow as a person.

- Further your career.

- Pursue your goals.

- Go solo travelling.

- Read more books.

- Connect with your local community.

- Continue finding your happiness and keep doing more of the things you love.

- Thrive in your singlehood, and enjoy this time while doing more work on you, for you.

Making Time For You

You might think you have all the time in the world, but it's imperative you make time for yourself. Choose yourself and put yourself first from time to time. That might mean you say no more often. You can say no to going to endless family functions. You can say no to meeting a friend because you want to go to a yoga class. You make time for yourself. Let's face it, even when we say we are putting ourselves first, it's actually about what we are doing with the time we have, and using it wisely.

Schedule in a meeting with yourself once a week where you check in with yourself. I call this the 'self-care meeting'. I set aside a few hours a week, and in this specified time, I do more of the things I love. I might light a candle, go for a walk, put on a face mask, dance or even listen to my favourite music, read a book, make a new dish. I find that it really is something I look forward too.

Things I've loved about singlehood:

- I like spending money on whatever I want, so if I want to buy another pair of heels I can.

14

- I like having a date with me, and spending a whole day in Waterstones reading books and drinking tea.

- I like having the bed to myself, and having a duvet and PJ day, watching back-to-back Punjabi and American movies, and rom coms.

- I like blasting bhangra tunes and a bit of Alicia Keys when I'm cooking.

- I spend more time in nature.

- I have learned how to cook.

- I have found new hobbies.

- I have made new friends.

- I have taken on projects in different cities.

- I have travelled more.

- I have worked on my own growth.

- I have taken time to understand myself.

- I have worked on past losses and heartbreaks.

MYTH #4

You Will Die Alone

You don't need rescuing

You don't need to settle for fear of being alone

You came into this world alone, and most likely will leave alone. Death itself is a mystery. Who knows where anyone ends up? Being a believer in God, my own opinion is that when my time on earth is complete, and I do come face to face with the creator, I want to smile, for I have lived my best life, with meaning and purpose. I followed my path, made my time on earth count, and faithfully fulfilled the dreams that God sowed in my heart.

There are millions of people across the world who die every day, from young children, to stillborn babies, to young adults who had their whole lives ahead of them, and possibly the next chapter to look forward to. Partners and children are left behind. This is the reality of life.

On my journey, I have had people say to me, 'Hurry up and get married, you will end up alone.' I've seen the worry in my parent's eyes too, as they age and wonder who will look after me if something happens to them. I would have days where my mind would play tricks on me and tells me i am not enough. This would cause anxiety. I felt lost in another world. I felt like I've disappointed my parents, that I'm afraid of getting older, and that I may lose my parents, they will die, and I will be on my own. The truth is, imperfection is impossible. It's painful to see my parents worry, and a lot of it is rooted in the culture I am from because marriage is so ingrained in us. I would rather be alone than with someone who isn't right for me. If it happens that I find that person, then that's great, but life is happening now, and I want to live. As for dying alone? Isn't that what happens anyway? No one stays here forever, so we might as well enjoy the journey.

Happiness is beating within us, it's just up to us to see it, seek it, and make our own memories. The change starts with me, with you. Now is the time to pave the way and make life beautiful for others. We can all make a difference. Don't be afraid to take risks, you never know where those opportunities can take you, and what you might learn about yourself. Embrace yourself as you are, the blemishes, the lines. After all, the plan wasn't to leave this place perfectly redesigning your imperfections into perfections, the plan was to leave with the skin that caught the sun, the hair that turned silver grey, to show that you have lived, embracing all the uncertainly, the highs and lows, beautifully, wildly-lived and won in this game called life.

MYTH #5

Single Parent

You are not a failure for giving something a go.
Your resilience is admirable.

Dear single parent,

Please take a bow. I salute you for rushing around to prepare dinner, getting the kids ready for school, doing the chores, holding down a job. If you can do all this without a partner, you are a force to be reckoned with.

If you choose to bring a child into this world, it is your responsibility to nurture and love them. Sadly, some environments can be controlling and toxic, but that can be true however many parents are around. A single parent can be an excellent role model, showing how to manage time,

19

manage money, take on responsibilities alone, and giving commitment to family.

A single parent family isn't necessarily a broken family.

Some tips for single parents:

- Involve the kids in your activities and get good at delegating small manageable tasks to children; they will love it.

- Discuss dreams and goals with your child(ren) and get them to commit to a good schedule that works for them. Introduce self care practices for them such as meditation, me time. Teach them to explore their hobbies and interests early on.

- Encourage open conversations and give lots of unconditional love Don't be hard on yourself, when you are doing the best you can.

Get them to help prepare meals, and plan activities with them. Not only will this help them feel loved but it will help you to not get overwhelmed. Even a simple thing as getting them to take it in turns to cook and wash up, and having a rota will help them to feel part of a mini project.

MYTH #6

You're Selfish

Prioritising yourself first does not make you selfish.

Selfish for what exactly? Choosing how to spend your disposable income after paying all your bills? For using this time to nurture your relationships with your family and siblings and close friends? Don't feel bad for prioritising you. Use this time to really get to know yourself, and pursue your hobbies, your goals and dreams. Remember you're not here to please anyone, or to seek validation from others. You're here to live to your rules, your standards.

How to deal with pressure and societal expectations

You get one shot at life. Your job isn't to please everyone else. Your job is to please yourself, so get better at listening to your intuition and follow your heart. It always knows what's right for you.

As a young girl, I lived in two different worlds. At school I was this obedient girl studying so hard to get good grades because I knew getting an education was the way to carve out a good life.

At home, I saw the differences in the roles of woman. I was expected to come home from school and help with the cooking and cleaning. I wasn't allowed out, or to date. It was not the done thing in my culture. I wasn't allowed to cut my hair, or wear short dresses or sleeveless tops until I was in my twenties.

Instead of marriage, my parents pushed education on to me and my four siblings, because they knew that is what would enable us to live feely and independently. It was expected in my culture, that women cooked and cleaned. My mother didn't get half the choices and privileges my parents gave me. My parents' dream was for me to study, and live the life they didn't get to live.

22

They still work so hard. That was my driver as a young girl, to give them the life they so deserve otherwise what good am I? They gave me the wings to let me fly, and carve a life I wanted on my terms and chase my dreams. I was the first woman in my family to be given choices. There's a fire in me, and this hunger for more and it all come back to my parents. They taught me the biggest lesson of life which is that I am enough and even when the outside world wants to drown me and tell me I am not, I look at their sacrifices and remind myself that everything I need is within me.

Even today my mother says she wishes she could speak English properly, she wishes she could drive a car, she wishes she had done more with her life. I look at her and see the dreams she didn't get to pursue, because she was busy raising five children. Yet here she is, she left her life back in Punjab to come to a new country and made a new life for herself.

The pressure of being a British Punjabi woman weighs me down. Some days it's the pressure I put on myself. My mind tells me I am not good enough and anxiety creeps in. Some days it's the pressure of life, this feeling that takes over my body telling me, 'You better hurry up, Sukhi, times running out.' Is there enough time for me to give my parents all the happiness they so deserve? For them to see me dressed as a Indian bride in my lengha, for me to become a mum? These are the days I remind myself that maybe this is my mission - to share this chapter, that I am meant to have this journey. That my faith and my mission and dreams are bigger then my fears. That this is the divine plan and no matter what I will keep trusting with every step I take that I am evolving. If this resonates with you, I am with you on this path. It's okay to be a little scared.

One of my aunties once said to my mum, 'My daughter-in-law is only twenty-three but there some girls out there who are nearly forty, they don't know what they want in life, don't even think about marriage and kids.' These stories used to upset me. It used to make me question myself. What have I done wrong? Why can't I find love? I would go to family functions, I tried online dating apps, speed dating events, but I didn't find love. I exhausted myself in the process, not realising I was putting pressure on myself and actually causing damage to myself. I was believing the voices in my head that told me I was not enough. I was degrading myself; I never practiced loving myself, love was something I gave to others, neglecting the love I deserved to give to myself. This was the biggest lesson I learnt –I don't need to take dating to seriously. I just need to be myself, and know what I want. I don't need to waste time getting to know someone or have meaningless conversations. If someone likes me then great! If not, that's fine too! I really need to understand the type of woman I am, what my needs and wants are and I need to nurture them wholeheartedly.

When it comes to other people's expectations, be clear about who you are. Don't be that people pleaser. Set yourself goals and shed layers that are no longer serving you. Whether that's putting up boundaries or removing toxic people from your life, do it, you're becoming a higher version of yourself. The most important thing is being honest with yourself about your needs and wants, and using this time to live your best life whilst becoming a self-reliant woman.

This doesn't mean my journey is smooth sailing. I felt pressured and sometimes still feel pressured by my parents who want me to settle down. There are different forms of pressure. In my case it's not pressure to get married, or forcing me to marry anyone because my parents will never do that to me. It's not even them making remarks at me, because if anything they have never made me feel bad for not being married as they understand how hard it is. It's an element of societal pressure, as what is a single Indian's woman's place if she does not get married? The only 'pressure' I see in my parent's eyes is the dream of seeing me get married. If you're in the same situation, don't take it to heart. Your parents only want to see you settled. Do speak to them calmy and ask them not to compare you to others, and to embrace the path that you're on. Encourage and reassure them and show them that you are happy and living your best life. They'll be happy seeing you happy.

MYTH #7

You're Immature

Your maturity is your super power

The real signs of immaturity are speaking badly about someone Mocking someone for being a singleton Being unaware of how the words you say to someone, especially to a single person, such as; 'you still haven't found anyone?' Or 'when will you have kids' can be really hurtful. Immature people are those who are ignorant of how these words can affect someone. Ultimately, we can all be immature from time to time, but there is a big difference between just being playfull and teasing someone and enjoying a few giggles, compared to purposefully antagonising someone to get a reaction, and to get your own entertainment.

I have met people younger than me who acted as though they were better than me just because they were already married and had children. One of the self-care rituals I started following was to stop comparing my path to others around me. You are not behind or ahead. You are exactly where you are meant to be for your path. Growth and maturity happen in different ways. Single people make important decisions all on our own.

MYTH #8

It's Your Fate

Create your own destiny. You are the master of your life

I have had people say that it must be my fate to be single. I must be suffering for some unknown reason and paying for sins I can't remember committing, maybe from a different life. Does that mean I was such an unfortunate soul in my last life that God has decided not to bless me with a loving husband and children in this one?

I don't think that's true.

I prioritised my career. Does that mean having the experiences I have had as a singleton of travelling, working abroad, and giving love to other people is my punishment? I don't think so.

I know why I am single - it's because I haven't met the right person. That doesn't mean I've stopped living, or that I am cursed.

Maybe it's not a punishment but a blessing in disguise. Perhaps you need to just look at it through a different lens. Singlehood is a choice not a punishment.

MYTH #9

You're Too Old

*Your age is just a number, it's the woman you
evolve to become*

I f you are over thirty and not yet married -
congratulations, you are on a journey to truly
get to know yourself.

You're not single because you've passed a
certain age. Love can happen at any time. You
haven't screwed up anything if you're living your
best life and doing all the great things you love.
You haven't screwed up, because happiness is
beating inside you, every minute, every second,
every day you're blessed to have; you've just got
to ensure you live your life based on your choices
and decisions.

31

You don't owe anyone an explanation. Life doesn't begin when you're rocking a diamond or a band on your finger. Your life is happening here and now, for you have a heart that's beating.

Being single over a certain age doesn't give people the right to ask why you aren't married. You don't see single people going up to married people asking why they are married. There are many paths to happiness. If you choose to get married in your fourth decade, or find love again in your fifth or even sixth decade, good for you. Do what makes you happy, and lights up your soul. If you find someone later and you just simply enjoy being together then that's perfectly fine too. Remember your age is just a number, it's about the person you are becoming.

What's the guarantee you even make it to old age? Or even wake up tomorrow? So the next time someone says 'You're too old now,' ask them, 'Too old for what? To live?'

MYTH #10

You Don't Know How To Date

There's too many rules around dating

Communicate your values and concentrate on planting the soils to creating the relationship you want

As a singleton, have you ever been told you're too available, that's why you're single? This was what my colleague said to me, and I didn't understand what she meant. She said I need to play hard to get, not be so forthcoming. That I had got dating all wrong. I shouldn't respond to a text message until seven hours later or agree to meet for a date so quickly. It was all so confusing. My personal opinion is, ditch the dating guides that instruct you to act like a "bitch" when you just need to be your real self. Listen to your heart. Life is busy as it is, and if you like someone and can meet them at a mutually convenient time, go for it. But if you were planning to go to the gym, or the evening class, or even meet a friend, you shouldn't rearrange your schedule.

If you like someone, and the conversation flows, continue making an effort, and make time for them. Don't be afraid to show them you care for them.

We are given a heart to love, so listen to your heart, and be yourself; that's how you open your heart up to receive.

Remember:

- Love isn't a game and don't let anyone play with your emotions.

- If a man is interested in you, pay attention not only to what he says but also his actions.

- If he's not interested or initiating contact or making an effort, move on, don't waste your time waiting for him to text you back!

- Don't play games, but don't be afraid to challenge him!

- Be your fun, playful self and the right people will naturally gravitate towards you.

Be your real self from the moment you meet him; you don't need to be someone else, you just need to be you.

MYTH #11

You're Not Putting Yourself Out There

It's never about putting yourself out there on multiple sites, and frantically matching with multiple people. It's more about meeting people naturally that will help you on your journey and growing your network.

One day after work, I meet a married friend for coffee. She's interested to know if there's any progress in my love life. When I tell her what I've been doing, she says, "Sorry, Sukhi, you're just not trying hard enough. You need to put yourself out there!"

Who can blame them for saying that when you haven't told them that you went to a professional mingle event last week? Or that you have secretly

36

joined three more matrimonial and dating sites. Or that you had a date with a hottie. In fact you had a ten-day romance with him but it fizzled out. Oh, they don't need to know all that, because nothing came of it, and they don't need to know either that a mutual friend introduced you to a guy, and he ghosted you, or about the one you met online who sounded so cute. The truth is maybe you're trying too hard. You're pushing yourself to make this happen, putting unnecessary pressure on yourself and, in the process, you're making yourself feel like shit, and you forget to pause to reflect on the amazing things you can do with your time and your life.

How, exactly, is a singleton meant to "put themselves out there?" How do they say they're available? Should they sign up for networking events? Join another app? Write a Facebook status – "I am single and looking to meet and mingle?" Maybe we're fed up of swiping, and going through the process of rejections, ghosting, men sending dick pics. Maybe we're fed up with opening emails asking for no strings attached sex. Maybe there are people like me who no longer want to put themselves on yet another site. Well, Sukhi, if you don't keep trying and putting yourself out there, how will you meet him? Well, readers, I don't know, maybe he will cross my path when I am no longer looking, and not attached to the outcome.

There have been times I paused on swiping, and attending events, and started doing more of the things I love. When I stopped worrying, I found I felt very different inside. The transformation shifted my mindset. I was enjoying my free time and enjoying my life! I did some fantastic things. I baked cupcakes for a charity, took part in a charity run, and I joined the gym. I went to a Sikh camp to learn more about spirituality.

I volunteered. I hiked, I travelled, I meditated. I went to the beach, visited cities, took holidays abroad. I learned so much more about myself. Sometimes it's good to stop trying, catch your breath, and still give yourself credit for how far you've come. These moments make my heart sing in so many ways and fill me with so much gratitude. I feel so fulfilled.

Tips on how to put yourself out there:

- New faces cross our path on a daily basis. So, keep an open mind.

- Reach out to your network.

- Join networking groups.

- Pursue new hobbies.

- Speak to new people that randomly cross your path.

There are many more ways of connecting with people other than dating apps. Don't be afraid to tell people you're open to introductions and keep an open mind.

MYTH #12

You're Not Beautiful Enough

Beauty isn't something that you apply, it's something that you already are

To be born is a miracle. A gift. The universe has crafted you and you are special. You have something to offer to the world, never forget that or think that you are not meant to be here. Tap into your gifts. You do not need to compare where you are or what you are to others.

Don't be the woman who envies what others have, the woman who sees other people's successes as her failures. Be the woman that builds mountains and supports the other women around you. You're the woman whose kindness spills out of you, because you know what it feels like when people have been unkind to you. You know what it feels like to silently cry. You're the woman who doesn't need to look at the things you lack or dislike your teeth, your hair, your nose, your height, your skin colour, but the woman who reminds herself that it's the inner beauty that radiates the most, when you are the woman you want to be. You're the woman that realises before we expect love to find us, in the coffee house, the train station or at work, that we need to turn inwards and fill our own cup so we overflow ourselves in love before we look to give love to others. You're the woman that knows she has everything within her. All the answers, the love, the guidance.

You might have been told you're too tall, too short, too fat, too skinny, too dark, too fair, petite, big-boned, you have small hips, big hips, you have a fat nose, a crooked nose.

I've had people reject me for not being beautiful enough, but it's okay, now looking back, they were not right for me, and I sincerely wish those people the best and hope that they find the right person for them. I actually pray for them. I forgive them. I know I am here for fleeting moments and I want to spend this time radiating love and kindness to the people I meet on my journey, because in my heart I have seen that when I do that it has changed my life. My mother always taught me to be kind and never to hurt anyone, because I have seen the way people can be unkind, and the impact that can have on someone. I realise that is not the woman I want to be, because I know it only hurts me in the process. I can let it go. I am so much more than my appearance, and I wouldn't want to be with someone because they thought I looked right. I realised that when I stopped looking for others to love me, and like me, I found it within me, my home. The home I nourish every day and I adore the woman I have become.

MYTH #13

You're Not Confident Enough

Real confidence is believing in yourself

A friend of mine was told that she needed to be more confident. Like me, she was independent, working away from home, living on her own, meeting friends and socialising. But apparently, when it comes to men, she's coming across as too shy. Well, who can blame her? Rocking up to a singles event on your own is enough to make anyone feel a bit nervous. That was not the reason she was single - some people are quiet, not reserved, and they still get married. Equally, those that are bubbly and loud might still be single. It has nothing to do with confidence.

It wasn't until I was well into my twenties that I started to feel more confident. I began experimenting with makeup, colouring my hair, and finding my self worth and who I was. Confidence and how you choose to perceive it is all down to perspective. I invested in finding mentors and the right people who can help me because that's what I needed, and now I am so much more confident in my skin, able to talk, and all that came with understanding who I was. It came with appreciating myself, taking time out to notice the woman I am. We all have the odd wobble, but confidence comes from trying new things, and celebrating the journey, the lessons, and taking a step back and asking, what I can learn from this?

Tips on how to be confident

- Don't be afraid to express your opinion.

- Be bold, be risky, be open. Talk to as many people as possible.

- Practice talking out loud in front of a mirror.

- Real confidence is knowing you you are! So, enjoy building the relationship with you, and get to know who you are. Record your own voice and listen to how you sound.

- If you are going to commit to something, give your all to it. Love for you, love for others, love for your life, love for the amazing things you have, love for the world. Always commit to it 100% otherwise don't do it.

MYTH #14

You're The Wrong Caste

Caste only divides us. Love and authenticity reunite us.

I f someone rejects you because of caste, then there is really nothing you can do to change that.

I personally don't believe in caste. I think it makes us judge each other and is something the older generation has carried forward. Is this something you want to take forward? Are we just blindly following tradition without questioning it? If someone rejects me because of my caste, then they're not the kind of person I want to be with. I want to be with someone who is much more open minded, and focused on growing together. I want unconditional love that's not bound by caste.

MYTH #15

You Fear Commitment

Don't water your fear so much that it becomes a tree and overtakes your whole life. When you let go of your fear, you welcome in new opportunities and experiences to create an amazing life.

I was told again and again that there was something wrong with me and that I must be afraid of settling down. But surely it's a good thing I have remained single because I know exactly what I am doing with my life? I see a lot of people that have entirely skipped dating and moved straight into marriage only to end up divorced or stuck in a marriage that they no longer want to be in.

You're not single because you fear commitment, you're single because you haven't met the right person. Marriage isn't something to tick off, and it can't be forced. It's better to wait, than marry wrong!

MYTH #16

You're Picky

Picky does not mean you are hard to please! it mean's you are selective and that's a good thing to be. Afterall, we do live in a world of 8 billion.

I 've lost count of the number of times I've been told I'm picky. This is a comment that even my mum will casually make.

"Picky" is the word thrown in by friends who want to help. But it's confusing – you're told to have a list, to be sure of what you're looking for, but also to "keep an open mind". The thing is, everyone has their definition of what they're looking for, I don't think that makes them picky, it's individual preference. Maybe you're just the right amount of picky.

So put all the bullshit dating advice to one side.

For example, I'm only five foot one. I wouldn't want to marry someone over six foot tall. However, a colleague thinks this makes me picky and that "it doesn't matter when you're lying down". But that's my individual preference, there is no right or wrong. So the next time someone asks if you're maybe just too picky, smile and say, 'Yeah, maybe I am,' and watch the colour drain.

When it comes to relationships, and finding the right person for you, I do believe you need to meet a variety of different people, otherwise how else will you know what you truly want in a relationship, from live, a partner even?

MYTH #17

You're Too Dark-Skinned

Your beauty is way beyond the colour of your skin. We are all worthy of love and to give love, it's already inside of us, we need to bring it out.

Someone told me once that they didn't want to date me because of my skin tone. I was mortified and somewhat shocked to hear this. The second time it happened, I was confused because I was open to getting to know this man and looking forward to date two. It didn't bother me that he was a few shades darker than me, and I was genuinely looking forward to a seeing him again because we had both been so nervous on the first date. So when he rejected me, to my face, and told me it wouldn't go anywhere, I was so upset. I went home and made a face mask of gram flour and honey, which promised me light skin. I washed my face, and, while my skin was glowing and refreshed, it wasn't any lighter. Then I cried to my mum and she told me to shut up and reassured me that I'm beautiful.

In Asian culture, growing up, I had seen how light skin was favoured and considered to be more beautiful, particularly for women. I'm so sorry if, like me, you were rejected for the color of your skin. I know how shit that feels. But never doubt your self-worth. You are beautiful. If someone doesn't want to be with you because of your skin color, they are definitely not the right person for you. Would you really want to be with someone who only likes you for your external beauty, rather than your internal values? I know that's that the person I want to spend my life with. My spiritual side tells me to see God in all, regardless of colour. And the type of man I want is someone that won't see my colour as a flaw or as the definition of my beauty.

MYTH #18

You're Stuck In The Past

Your energetic vibration is everything. When you are replaying the old movie in your mind about the last heartbreak, or the times you felt people have let you down. You are only stopping yourself and missing out on the wonderful opportunities that lie ahead. Trust your path and embrace this healing journey. It's crucial because you are about to level up!

You're transitioning. You might have had your heart broken, or the person you wanted to marry has married someone else, whatever the reason, I understand the pain of letting go. You're not single because of this, though. Heartbreak's a hard one to navigate but I promise you this time will pass too. You will return to yourself. What a waste it would be to deny yourself happiness, whatever that might be, because of a past relationship. You might not be looking for another relationship, but that doesn't mean your life is meaningless because there still other beautiful things you can pursue. Don't put your life on hold, you will waste valuable days, months, and years. I admit there have been times in my journey when I didn't like the single life. I let it consume me, rob me of my sleep, my peace.

My advice if you are going through a heartbreak is:

- delete their number and get rid of all presents; and all emails, and messages.

- run yourself an indulgent bubble bath;

- go away on a trip somewhere alone;

- delete their pictures;

- talk about your feelings with a close friend;

- stop looking at their social media;

- find new passions;

- don't rush to get into another relationship - take your time to heal;

- take time to validate your feelings;

- buy a journal and get writing;

- never be afraid to get the help you need to deal with any deep-rooted trauma.

Embrace this chapter, and the heartbroken you. Create space in your life, and know that you are enough. You are whole. Dealing with heartbreak means knowing that when you lose yourself in this chaos, you will find yourself. It's knowing and accepting that it might be the end of the relationship, but it really is the beginning of you. It's knowing that you will have days when your heart shatters and breaks into pieces. It's knowing you will have days where you will struggle to talk, and get out of bed, where the mere thought of whoever caused this reduces you to tears. You might never get answers or closure. You might never get the apology you deserve. Forgive yourself for pouring love into someone who had no intention of loving you back. Forgive yourself for not knowing better. Forgive them for their mistakes. This will set you free. Let it go, and know that you will be okay. Even when you hit rock bottom, the dark place where you see no light or hand to help you. This is the moment where you find yourself and become whole again. This is when you rise like a phoenix. Believe me when I say this -you will overcome this. You will become stronger. You will step into the new woman and reclaim your power. Don't ever think that nothing beyond this moment will ever be sweeter or richer. Have faith in yourself, and your journey. Take the time to get the healing you need. To become more grounded. Look after your mental and physical and emotional wellbeing.

If you are trying to make someone yours chances are they aren't the one- all the video's I've seen about 10 ways to make him text you back, its all untrue in my opinion, love doesn't work like that. These video's are not a magic pill, you don't need to cast spells to make them yours, or wait for them to make you feel special. Love doesn't work like that, no one can make you feel enough and whole only you can feel that yourself. When your with the right person, you feel a sense of unconditional love and belonging. They feel like home. Love and the right person doesn't make you feel like you're scared, or inadequate. Staying in relationship, or even a friendship, or something when it hurts is not love, they suppose to energize and excite you not drain you. When on the road to healing, you just need to be you and you will attract the right people when you show up as you.

The past does not define you, always remember that when you find yourself floating back in time.

It's an important reminder to know that Mr right even when he comes can't be everything. Sometimes, we put so many expectations on our partner, not realising that they can't fill you up in all the ways you want them too. He can't give you everything.

As much as it hurts, the past is done and dusted. The chapter is done. You can cry as much as you want, but if they wanted to be in your life, they would be. Acceptance is such beautiful thing. Know that from this point onwards, you can move forward. Know that you are okay. You will be okay. Accept that they were your biggest teacher and that you can gracefully let them go and send them love, healing, light and blessings. You can still be successful at your own pace and timeline.

I do feel that it takes longer for women to overcome heartbreak. The time to overcome this can vary from woman to woman. Take the time to rebuild yourself before finding another relationship. Often, we think that to overcome the last relationship we must rush to find another partner. The healing journey in between is the most crucial. Imagine rushing to find another partner, only to not bring your best self into that relationship, expecting the other person to fix you, and help you overcome the pain. This is obviously not fair on the other person, as they are not your therapist. I recall a time I went on a date with a man who was pouring his heart out about his last relationship. This was a red flag for me! A cry for help, which I am not able to fix. The lesson I learnt was, the focus is never to fix them, as they need to take personal responsibility for that. The real focus was to concentrate on building a great relationship with the right person. Another interesting thing I learnt from this experience was the focus shouldn't be on wanting to know about the other person's past relationships, instead it's on planting the seeds of what I want. I also learnt that to really want a great relationship, you must heal from the past, and having been on the receiving end of listening to this, I learnt the importance of communicating my boundaries.

MYTH #19

You Don't Know How To Date

When going on a date, be relaxed and enjoy getting to know each other

What does that mean? That's like saying, mate, you suck. You're a flop. Like you don't know how to kiss? Are you boring? What exactly does it mean?

You will get rejected, and ghosted; you will receive inappropriate messages from losers, people who don't reply to your emails, people who question you; well, let them! Yes, you will get that ache in your stomach when you're attending everyone else's wedding, whilst wondering where your significant other is. Yes, you might go to your friends', cousins', even your neighbour or colleague's baby shower for the second time, and you might be asked, 'Have you found anyone yet?' You might be worrying about your biological clock, or the fact that you're at your colleague's second wedding, whilst you're still swiping on the apps. This happened to me, but that's their journey, and I am on my journey.

I've read a lot of advice from dating gurus and have found nothing of value. The essential thing you need to know about dating is just be your authentic self. Be the things you look for - be kind, smile, don't be so serious, dating is meant to be fun, like two friends hanging out. Be compassionate, it helps to build a connection, and if you both feel like there is something there, then great, if not, you haven't lost anything.

The first time I got ghosted, I took it really personally. My advice is, before you embark on the roller coaster journey of online dating, accept that you will get ghosted. You will be rejected; you will get slow responses. You will encounter people who send you two replies back and then disappear. You will meet people who cancel on you. You will meet people who will take your number and they may never call you. You will even get people who message you once, or keep on messaging you and they can be talking to several people at any one time. Be prepared and don't put all your eggs in one basket. In fact, I would encourage you to talk to multiple people at any one time.

How to deal with people who ghost you

Delete and block their number. You're not married to them, they are an acquaintance, a stranger. Don't waste your time seeking an answer from them, or even closure. The proof is in their actions; get good at observing and spotting people's actions and lack of effort. The simple reason they didn't call, text, or arrange a date is that they didn't want to.

Remember, a failed date is not a failed life. It is not a reflection on you. You're going to be okay. You are already okay!

MYTH #20

You're Too Positive and Happy All The Time

The world doesn't need more negativity. The world needs more people who are filled with a positive outlook. Be the light in the world, not the storm.

There is a stigma that single people are cynical, sad, frustrated, and alone, so being told once that I was single because I was too positive and happy was baffling. Having a positive outlook was now apparently working against me. Once, when I caught up with a friend for lunch, I was asked why I was smiling and positive. My friend was expecting me to be a wreck because I hadn't yet found a husband. I was okay with being single.. What I found though, was my friend was not. She had an issue with me being positive. Maybe she expected me to be complaining about how shit my life was. Or perhaps that helped her feel better because she was spinning plates managing her two kids. For the first time in a long time, I felt great, but sometimes other people aren't happy to see that you're positive and feeling significant.

Tips to stay positive and feel significant:

- The down days will come. On these days acknowledge that it's a tough day.

- Prioritise you. Check in with yourself, simply by asking 'how am I feeling?

- Have self-care rituals to uplift and change your mood.

- Have a little dance. It sounds silly, but I always feel better once I have had a little dance.

- Have boundaries– you don't have to continue to see people like this. Don't forget to remind yourself that singlehood is a valid option, whilst continuing to live your best life.

- There might be moments where you feel invisible and insignificant because you aren't married, and you don't have a plus one, or children. You might get anxious about attending family functions, even feel these emotions when you see other people you know who have children, and they may be showing off which is hurtful. My advice is just focus on your own path. I wouldn't even feel the need to talk about it as its wasted energy.

- Focus on the things you can control and channel your energy into your dreams, your hobbies, your passions. Don't compare, keep the faith. You don't need to please others, you just need to pursue more of the things that make you happy. If other people say things, it's a reflection on them, not you.

- Speak up and be significant; you are important so don't be afraid to be loud, and be yourself.

Happiness has nothing to do with feeling sad sometimes. True self love is really embracing all of your journey- saying nice things to yourself, treating yourself, and true beauty is simply being the women you want to be, and look like. You're the true warrior, a women who rises, shatters, loses herself, but she learns to climb again. Embrace it, be louder, that simply be with you, this version of you, sit with her, nurture and talk to her. You are evolving, before you step into the newer you, just enjoy this moment of this version of you. Don't be afraid of falling, of failing. Know that you're a goddess, now that you have the power within you, that you have barely emerged yet, so start enjoying your life and the journey more. You're the master of your life.

MYTH #21

You're Intimidating

To the right person, you won't be intimidating.
You are only perceived intimidating to the
wrong people

I was told that having a career and travelling so much could work against me. I have spent a reasonable amount of time working away, which has meant travelling alone, and living alone. I was happy to eat alone in my hotel room, to venture into restaurants alone. I was actually happier doing this than eating out with colleagues.

This did perhaps give the impression that I either had no friends or that I was unapproachable. But neither is true, I'm just happy in my own company. And how am I meant to show that I'm not intimidating? Do I need to act needy? Surely if I can hold down a job, drive, and have some respect for myself, those are great qualities to bring to a marriage. If both of us are financially independent, we are both helping to build a great future, the only real discussion and compromise are about who is doing the washing up, and peeling the potatoes for dinner. If we can both do that, then that's the icing on the cake.

According to my colleague, the past decade of being single has led to me being far too liberal. I might have sabotaged my chances of getting a ring on my finger. According to him, going on holiday every year, plus going out to restaurants, while building my career, has messed up my chances. 'Trust me, Sukhi, people will think you're too outgoing and liberal.' What would you expect a thirty-something woman to have done with her life?

Be with someone that makes you feel appreciated, supported and an equal.

MYTH #22

You're Outspoken

Outspoken does not mean you become timid or quiet. Be the right amount of challenging. Express your thoughts and opinions. The right person will value this and not see you as outspoken

If you're outspoken, then you're doomed. You might as well forget finding a husband. Are you considered blunt for having an opinion? If someone wants you to be suppressed and not speak up, do you want to be with them?

Never be afraid to share your opinions, your perspectives, your thoughts. After all, the goal is to feel an equal in a relationship. You want to find your voice and to be able to express yourself freely - that is the true essence of inner peace and happiness.

How to deal with married friends that don't want to prioritise you or check in with you.

This is a tough one. I was on the phone with a friend once, upset and needing to talk. Midway through the conversation, she told me she had to go now because her husband was home, and she was cooking him chicken tikka. She didn't text me back, or call me; a whole month went past, and when she did next call, it was all about her and her nagging mother-in-law. Often, on this journey, I have had married friends say to me, you don't know how busy I am, I have numerous family gatherings on. They were really saying "I don't want to check in with you and hear about your miserable life", and sadly that's how I lost some friends. They just fizzled out, kind of like a few of my dates. Single life doesn't mean your life is not busy enough or exciting enough. In fact, I've found it to be the opposite at times. I have had to learn to spin plates on my own, and I've learned how to deal with spiders!

Personally, I feel that sometimes people are removed from your life because they are no longer serving you. Or they came to teach you something, and now have to leave so that you can meet new people on your journey, people who will help you learn even more things about yourself. The harsh reality of life is sometimes we deny the people that want to get to know us, that actually want us, and want to spend time with us and check in with us, because we are too busy trying to get that love and attention from someone that doesn't even want to make an effort. This is where you get good at wishing those people well and not getting too attached. The reality is it does become difficult to maintain close friendships once those friends are married because they too are entering a new world with responsibilities, and friendships naturally evolve. Some friends last a life time, some change, some drop off your radar, some will make the effort, some will not prioritise or check in. It's up to you to find out which ones are the ones worth keeping.

DON'T

- wallow in self-pity.

- compare your path to others.

- question yourself.

- curse yourself.

- cry about it.

DO

- live your best life - start now right, this moment;

- embrace and find beauty in every day and every moment;

- fill your schedule with the things you love;

- find your purpose, your passion;

- find your inner peace and joy - follow your heart;

- let go of any beliefs, people, and thoughts that no longer serve you.

- invest in the people that invest you in

- keep meeting new people that challenge you, help you to think differently and bring new ways of doing things, having fun so that you continue to grow and evolve.

TOXIC PEOPLE

We've all had toxic people in our lives - the person who dims our light, isn't fun to be around, is miserable, lets us down, drags us down, upsets us repeatedly. Be very selective about who you let into your life, and who you give your time and energy to. Give your love to the right people; those who are worthy of it.

How to deal with toxic people:

- Ignore them.

- Don't give them permission to prey into your personal life, offend you, or mock you for your choices. Don't be afraid to tell them if they offend you.

- Have good people in your circle that care for you.

- You can say, "It's none of your business."

- Do not tolerate bullying or suffer in silence. Find your voice.

- Don't feel compelled to stay in a toxic environment. You are only one step away from a different life and making a different choice. Remember that.

- Remove them from your life and replace them with better people.

WHAT IF YOU STAY SINGLE FOREVER?

S o what? Isn't it better to be single than to be in a loveless relationship? I would rather be single than marry the wrong person. I've travelled to twenty-six countries, worked abroad, travelled business class, and lived in different cities. I would not have been able to do any of that if I was married. I probably wouldn't have made it to the next town.

I've actually learned what it meant to nurture the relationships I have and value the people I do have in my life, rather than worry about the ones that aren't.

My advice is if you want to do something, do it. If you want to go hiking, travel to Australia on a solo trip or volunteer in India, or go on a retreat or learn a new language, learn to speak Spanish, then do it! Enhance your own life.

Meditation helped me to become aware of my inner critic. It taught me that actually, I need to be mindful of my emotions, listen to the feelings behind them, and ask what the root cause was. It taught me that I can seek help; there are professionals out there if I want to talk to a therapist. Meditation taught me self-awareness and allowed me to go inwards; it taught me gratitude for all the things I have. It helped me to sit with my thoughts, in stillness. It taught me to learn more about myself, who I am; it taught me to love myself. Singlehood has allowed me to learn more about me and appreciate the woman I have become, and I am excited to see what the next decade will bring.

CONCLUSION

You're okay the way you are. You don't need to prove anything to anyone. You don't need to live with other people's expectations, you just need to live your life. Reread these words. Your life is about your choices, your decisions. You don't want to live a life of regret for all the things you wanted to do, but you never did, so prioritise you. Find your voice and your backbone.

You get one life, don't waste it questioning, wallowing in self-pity. I say this sincerely because I used to be that person. I used to feel a lack of self-worth and felt like I wasn't good enough. I used to not like myself sometimes, and I didn't feel worthy of a relationship. Where do you want your life to go? If you don't want to get married and have kids, these are the choices you make for you. It's your life.

Be the authentic you. Now is the time to find your voice and be the person you have always wanted to be. Step into her. Now is the time to take care of yourself, and nourish yourself. Love yourself just a little bit more each day, and enjoy getting to know yourself a little bit more.

Whatever path you find yourself on, whether you are single by choice, or simply because you haven't found the right person, or you are dating, and meeting people, simply be happy. Choose you.

Wake up feeling excited about life, energised and raring to go! Remember too that it's okay to lose yourself, it's okay to cry, it's okay to have your heart broken. It's okay to embrace those dark times and forgive yourself for not knowing better. We all make mistakes, we all face tough times, we all question other people's actions thinking we are perfect, but we are more similar then we think. Don't waste your life living in the past dwelling on things you can't change. Instead pay attention to the road ahead. Appreciate your journey, and cherish it, for it's made you into a strong, confident, joyful, independent woman.

You may go on to find your soul mate, you may not, but whatever happens, you will carve out a path for yourself. It's your story, your way, find beauty in your journey.

ABOUT THE AUTHOR

SUKHI KAUR is a British writer of Indian heritage. She resides in England, the UK. Sukhi loves to write, travel, exercise and cook. She likes to meet new people and is passionate about redefining singlehood, and sharing her story through her books and blogs. You can connect with her on social media platforms.

OTHER BOOKS BY THE AUTHOR

Why Aren't You Married Yet?

Why Aren't You Married Yet is a memoir of the author's journey. It explores navigating the British Indian Culture, growing up, the corporate world, success, sisterhood, family, love, falling apart, resilience, and personal and spiritual growth. Sukhi Kaur paves the way to redefine singlehood, becoming a much needed voice to empower woman to carve out and live their best life. A must read!

Extracts From The Book....

- CHAPTER 6: 2010 - The Yellow Ferrari

- CHAPTER 7: 2012 - Are You Picky?

- CHAPTER 11: 2014 - Shenanigans at Work

- CHAPTER 12: Going Online

STAY IN TOUCH

You have reached the end of my book, and I want to thank you for going on this journey with me.

You have allowed me to share an important part of my journey, which has made me the woman I am today.

I would love to hear from you! Please connect with me on:

Connect with Sukhi online at:

Website: www.sukhi-kaur.co.uk

Instagram:
https://www.instagram.com/evolve_coaching0
1/

Facebook:
https://www.facebook.com/SukhiKaurUK

Twitter: https://twitter.com/EvolveCoaching6

Pinterest:

https://www.pinterest.co.uk/sukhi_kaur01/_saved/

I would be very grateful if you can leave me a review on Kindle and Amazon. You can find the link here:

Thank you so much, and look forward to connecting with you.

Printed in Great Britain
by Amazon

60273808R00056